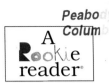

A
Rookie
reader®

A Lunch With Punch

Written by Jo S. Kittinger

Illustrated by Jack Medoff

Children's Press®
A Division of Scholastic Inc.
New York • Toronto • London • Auckland • Sydney
Mexico City • New Delhi • Hong Kong
Danbury, Connecticut

For Joan Broerman with thanks
for her friendship and encouragement
—J.S.K.

To Lynn and Zack
—J.M.

Reading Consultants

Linda Cornwell
Literacy Specialist

Katharine A. Kane
Education Consultant
(Retired, San Diego County Office of Education
and San Diego State University)

Library of Congress Cataloging-in-Publication Data
Kittinger, Jo S.
  A lunch with punch / written by Jo S. Kittinger ; illustrated by Jack
Medoff.– 1st American ed.
      p. cm. – (Rookie reader)
Summary: A boy packs his lunch with delicious items, and then shares it
with a friend who has forgotten his own lunch at school.
   ISBN 0-516-22879-X (lib. bdg.)   0-516-27785-5 (pbk.)
   [1. Sharing–Fiction. 2. Food–Fiction. 3. Stories in rhyme.] I.
Medoff, Jack, ill. II. Title. III. Series.
   PZ8.3.K65637Lu 2003
   [E]–dc21
                              2003003762

CHILDREN'S PRESS, and A ROOKIE READER®, and associated logos are trademarks and or
registered trademarks of Scholastic Library Publishing. SCHOLASTIC and associated logos
are trademarks and or registered trademarks of Scholastic Inc.
1 2 3 4 5 6 7 8 9 10 R 12 11 10 09 08 07 06 05 04 03

I pack my lunch.

Peanut butter
on bread.

Add some jelly,
thick and red.

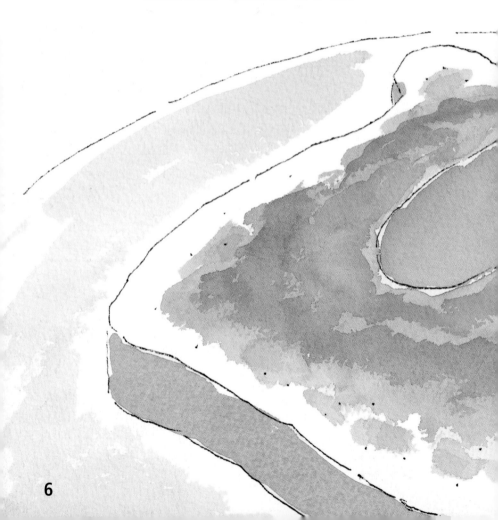

7

Money for milk.

Dimes and a nickel.

A bunch of grapes.

14

A sour pickle.

A pudding cup.

Carrots to crunch.

DISCARD

20

Crackers for a snack.

Cookies to munch.

Juice or punch?

Punch is fine.

Zack forgot his lunch.

Come share mine!

Word List (46 words)

a	fine	munch	snack
add	for	my	some
and	forgot	nickel	sour
bread	grapes	of	thick
bunch	his	on	to
butter	I	or	with
carrots	is	pack	Zack
come	jelly	peanut	
cookies	juice	pickle	
crackers	lunch	pudding	
crunch	milk	punch	
cup	mine	red	
dimes	money	share	

About the Author

Jo S. Kittinger, a native of Florida, lived in several states before settling in Alabama. A love of books and a passion to create inspires Jo to write both fiction and nonfiction books for children. Jo enjoys pottery, photography, and reading in her spare time. While teaching her own children to read, Jo realized the critical role of emergent readers.

About the Illustrator

Jack Medoff's cartoons have appeared in magazines, newspapers, advertisements, and commercials. He has also illustrated books for children and website cartoons. His work is on exhibit in galleries in Westport, Connecticut, and Rockport, Massachusetts. Jack has also worked as an art director for advertising agencies in New York and Los Angeles. He lives in Weston, Connecticut, with his wife, Lynn, his son, Zack, and his iguana, Zeke.